BRANCH LINES TO CLACTON AND WALTON

Vic Mitchell

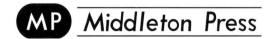

MP Middleton Press

Front cover: Class 3P 4-4-2T no. 41936 stands in the bay platform at Colchester on 25th August 1956 with a local train bound for Clacton-on-Sea. (B.Pask)

Back cover upper: Class J15 0-6-0 no. 65543 stands at the up platform at Colchester on 15th November 1959. An island platform now stands on the right. (Colour-Rail.com.)

Back cover lower: Inside Clacton Maintenance Depot on 21st December 1993 is a track tamping machine, plus two class 312 EMUs. They carry boards stating NOT TO BE MOVED and are numbered 312711 and 312710. (D.A.Pollock)

Published September 2011

ISBN 978 1 908174 04 8

© Middleton Press, 2011

Design Deborah Esher

Published by
    Middleton Press
    Easebourne Lane
    Midhurst
    West Sussex
    GU29 9AZ
Tel: 01730 813169
Fax: 01730 812601
Email: info@middletonpress.co.uk
www.middletonpress.co.uk

Printed in the United Kingdom by Henry Ling Limited, at the Dorset Press, Dorchester, DT1 1HD

INDEX

ACKNOWLEDGEMENTS

I am very grateful for the assistance received from many of those mentioned in the credits, also to A.R.Carder, P.R.Chappell, R.R.Clow, G.Croughton, J.B.Horne, S.C.Jenkins, G.Kenworthy, N.Langridge, B.Lewis, C.Phillips, Mr D. and Dr S. Salter and, in particular, my wife who has meticulously typeset my scribblings for 30 years. Included in my appreciation is Chris Cock who has kindly supplied data from the Bryan Wilson Signalling Register.

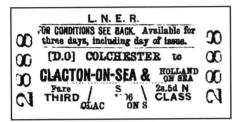

Routes in the Tendring Hundred area in the 1930s. At the top is the Harwich branch, which features in the *Branch Lines to Harwich and Hadleigh* album. (Railway Magazine)

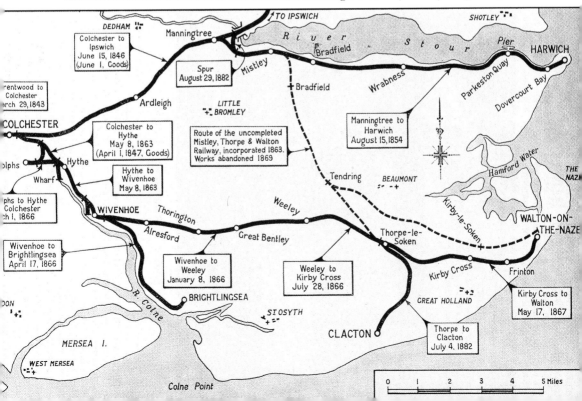

GEOGRAPHICAL SETTING

The routes traverse an area known as the Tendring Hundred, a medieval term. It occupied the area between the River Stour and the River Colne, with the small village of Tendring near its centre.

Most of the district is less than 100ft above sea level and the coastal area has low cliffs, which have attracted many miles of residential development, particularly for retirement homes. The coast is also noted for its Martello Towers and its extensive holiday accommodation.

Colchester is of Roman origin and has developed as an important trading and strategic centre, complete with a castle and, since the 1850s, has been a garrison town of great importance. All the lines are within the county of Essex.

The maps are to the scale of 25ins to 1 mile, with north at the top, unless otherwise indicated.

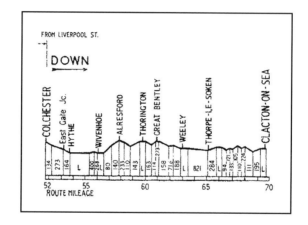

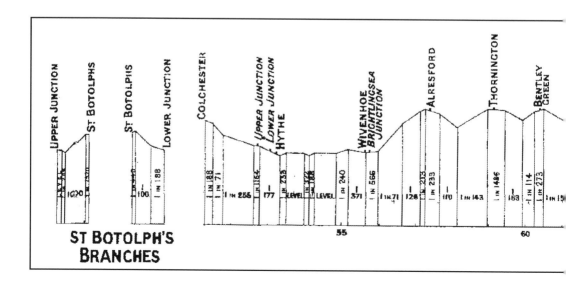

ST BOTOLPH'S
BRANCHES

HISTORICAL BACKGROUND

Colchester received Eastern Counties Railway trains from London, when its section from Brentwood opened on 29th March 1843.

The Eastern Union Railway opened between Colchester and Ipswich on 15th June 1846. The Colchester, Stour Valley, Sudbury & Halstead Railway added a short freight branch south to Hythe on 1st April 1847. All three companies became constituents of the Great Eastern Railway in 1862. An Act on 13th August 1858 enabled the Tendring Hundred Railway to build a line from Hythe to Wivenhoe and trains were operated by the GER between Colchester and Wivenhoe from 18th May 1863. Services were extended to Weeley on 8th January 1866, to Brightlingsea on 18th April 1866, to Kirby Cross on 28th July 1866 and to Walton-on-the-Naze on 17th May 1867. The Brightlingsea branch was built by the Wivenhoe & Brightlingsea Railway and operated by the GER, except from 1st August 1876 until 1st September 1877, when the former used its own stock. It sold out to the latter in 1893.

The branch from Thorpe-le-Soken to Clacton-on-Sea opened on 4th July 1882, its Act having been dated 2nd August 1877. The THR was taken over by the GER on 29th June 1883. A notably destructive earthquake took place in Colchester in 1884.

The GER became part of the London & North Eastern Railway in 1923 and this formed most of the Eastern Region of British Railways upon nationalisation in 1948.

Following severe flood damage, the Brightlingsea branch was closed from 1st February 1953 until 7th December of that year. The route closed to all traffic on 15th June 1964.

The remaining lines became part of Network SouthEast on 10th June 1986. Privatisation resulted in the routes being branded First Great Eastern on 5th January 1997 when FirstBus was awarded a 7¼ year franchise. This became First Group, but the operation was transferred to National Express, which applied the meaningless name of 'one' from 1st April 2004. It was renamed National Express East Anglia in 2008. In recent years, the routes have been branded "The Sunshine Coast Line".

Electrification

The Colchester to Clacton and Walton sections were electrified before the main line, a partial local service starting on 16th March 1959, to prove the new 25 kV AC system. The gap between Chelmsford and Colchester saw some electric trains from 18th June 1962, with the full service starting 12 months later. Colchester to Ipswich followed on 13th May 1985.

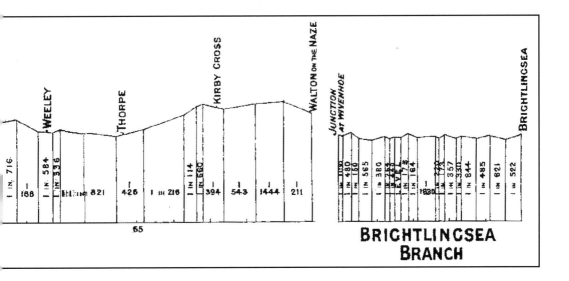

BRIGHTLINGSEA
BRANCH

PASSENGER SERVICES

After completion to Walton, the timetable offered 3(0) trips, but in 1869 it showed 6(1) trains (the figures in brackets are the Sunday frequencies). The services for December 1870 were 3(0). In June 1883, the Walton numbers were 6(2) and Clacton was the same, but with 1(2) extras running just from Walton to Clacton. The figures were similar in 1890, but without the short workings. The Brightlingsea branch had similar frequencies, but no up trains on Sundays in 1890. It had started with 3(0).

By the Summer of 1903, there were 10(8) to Walton and 14(5) to Clacton. The latter had a 1.04am arrival on Sundays, called the "Supper Train" (12.03 from Liverpool Street). Brightlingsea had 11(5).

The 1910 timetable showed the 1.56pm express to Felixstowe slipping coaches at Colchester at 3.02, the Clacton portion arriving at 3.40. The other figures were 16(6); the former included 2 to Clacton from Walton. Brightlingsea had 13(3) and Walton received 20(8), this including 2 on weekdays from Clacton. A regular interval service, with hourly buffet cars, began in 1950. Below are sample timetables prior to electrification. The trial electric 1959 timetable brought an erratic service, with two trains in most hours, but with 14 to Brightlingsea. However, this was daily. By June 1963, the London service and the local ones were both hourly, the latter running via St. Botolphs. A similar service has been maintained since, but with fewer through trains to Walton.

October 1923

COLCHESTER, BRIGHTLINGSEA, WALTON-ON-NAZE, and CLACTON-ON-SEA.—L. & N. E.

COLCHESTER, BRIGHTLINGSEA, CLACTON-ON-SEA, and WALTON-ON-THE-NAZE.—Great Eastern.

	mrn	mrn	mrn	mrn	aft	aft	aft	aft	mrn	aft		Up.	mrn	mrn	mrn	mrn	aft	aft	aft	aft	aft	mrn	aft
London 134 dp	5 10		7 8		10 0			5 30	8 2	1015		Walton-on-Naze	8	9 53		1058	1150	1250 2 45		5 10 6 28		1040 5	
Colchester...dep	6 55	9 27		1121		2 17 4 40		6 55		1025		Frinton-on-Sea	8 12 9 57		1057	1134 1258 2 49		5 15 6 33		1044 5 11	
St. Botolph's		9 37	1115			2 27 4 50	6 57			1029		Kirby Cross	8 16		11 1 1138 1258 2 53		5 18 6 37		1048 5 15	
Hythe	7 12 7 30 9 41	1119	a		2 31 4 54 7 17	10			1035		Thorpe...arr	8 22 10 4		11 7 1144 1 4 3 59		5 24 6 43		1054 5 21	
Wyvenhoe...arr	7 20 7 43 9 46	1125 1135		2 36 4 59 7 7	7 15					Clacton-on-SeaA dp	8 18 9 55		1055	1255 2 53		5 17 6 35		5 12	
Wyvenhoe ...dep	7 50 7 50 9 50	1138 1148		3 40 5 3 7 19 7 19						Thorpe...arr	8 22 10 4		11 5	1 43 2		5 26 6 44		5 21	
Brightlingsea.ar	8 5 8 5 10 5	1153 1153		2 55 5 15 7 34 7 34						Thorpe ...dep	8 27 10 9		1110	1 93 9		5 32 6 50		5 23	
Wyvenhoe ...dep	7 27	9 48	1136		2 38 5 1		7 17	1036			Weeley	8 33 1015		1116	1 153 15		5 38 6 56		5 29	
Alresford	7 32	9 53			2 43 5 6		7 22	1041			Great Bentley	8 38		1121	1 203 20		5 43 7 1		5 34	
Thorington	7 45	9 58			2 48 5 11		7 27	1046			Thorington	8 42 1022		1126	1 243 24		5 47 7 5		5 39	
Great Bentley	Slg.	10 2			2 52 5 15		7 31	1050			Alresford	8 46		1130	1 323 32		5 51 7 10		5 43	
Weeley	8 10	1015			2 58 5 21		7 37	1055			Wyvenhoe ...arr	8 50 1028		1134	1 323 32		5 55 7 14		5 47	
Thorpe ...arr	8 17	1020		1156	3 3 5 26		7 42	11 1			Brightlingsea..d	8 30 1010 1018		1120	1 293 25 35		7 55			
Thorpe ...dep	8 23	1023		1156	3 5		7 46	11 3			Wyvenhoe...arr	8 45 1024 1023		1135	1 303 30 45		8 10			
Clacton-on-Sea ar	8 45	1032		12 7	3 15 5 37		7 55	1112			Wyvenhoe ...dep	8 52 1029 1035		1135	1 343 34 5 48 5 57 7 16 8 17				5 46	
Thorpe ...dep	8 25	1025		12 0 1 16	3 20 5 42		8 0	1117			Thorpe...arr	8 48 1025 1041		1145	1 403 40 5 55 6 3 7 22 6 25				6 2	
Kirby Cross	8 54	1031		1210 1 27	3 29 5 43		7 55	1122			St. Botolph's (152)	9 5		1044	1 483 45 5 58 6 11 7 29				6 8	
Frinton-on-Sea	9 0	1036		1210 1 27	3 29 5 45		8 0	1117			Colchestr 137,134	9 12 1040		1145	1 533 45 6 18 7 36 8 4				6 10	
Walton-on-Naze a	9 5	1039		1213 1 30	3 23 5 45		8 5	1120			London 137 ar	1020 1215			2 23 5 50		8 09 5		8 0	

February 1890

April 1943

COLCHESTER, BRIGHTLINGSEA, FRINTON-ON-SEA
WALTON-ON-NAZE, and CLACTON-ON-SEA

Week Days

	mrn	mrn	mrn	mrn	mrn	mrn	mrn	mrn		aft	aft E	aft S	aft S		aft E	aft S	aft S	aft
3 London (LiverpoolSt) dep	4 33				8 12	8 15		10 0		11 20		1235			1 0	1 30		2 15
Colchester...dep	6 45	7 9		8 7	9 47	1021	1038	12 7		1 42		1 58	2 6		2 46	2 56		4 15
St. Botolph's arr	6 51				9 53	1027												4 21
St. Botolph's dep	7 2		7 57		9 57	1031			1215	1 35		1 49					3 0	4 25
Hythe	7 6 7 14	8 1	8 12		10 1	1035	1043	1212	1219	1 39	1 47 1 53		2 11			3 7	4 29
Wivenhoe arr	7 11 7 19	8 6	8 17		10 6	1040	1048	1217	1224	1 44	1 52 1 58	2 6	2 16		2 54	3 43	3 12	4 34
Wivenhoe ...dep	7 24	8 10			10 7		1053		1225	1 57		2 11			3 0		3 13	4 40
Brightlingsea arr	7 36	8 22			1019		11 5		1237	2 9		2 23			3 12		3 25	4 52
Wivenhoe ...dep	7 20		8 18			1049	1218			1 53		2 7	2 17		2 56	3 6		4 35
Alresford	7 26		8 24			1055				1 59			2 23					4 41
Thorington	7 30		8 28			1059				2 3			2 27					4 45
Great Bentley	7 34		8 32			11 3				2 7			2 31		3 5	3 15		4 49
Weeley	7 39		8 37			11 8				2 12			2 36					4 54
Thorpe-le-Soken arr	7 43		8 41			1112	1232			2 16		2 21	2 40		3 13	3 24		4 58
Thorpe-le-Soken...dep	7 49		8 47			1118	1242			2 27		2 27 2 44			3 24	3 31		5 4
Kirby Cross	7 55		8 53			1124	1249			2 33		2 33 2 52			3 30	3 37		5 10
Frinton-on-Sea	8 0		8 57			1129	1254			2 38		2 38 2 56			3 35	3 42		5 14
Walton-on-Naze arr	8 2		9 0			1132	1257			2 41		2 41 2 59			3 38	3 45		5 17
Thorpe-le-Soken ...dep	7 45		8 43			1114	1234			2 18		2 23 2 42			3 15	3 27		5 0
Clacton-on-Sea A arr	7 54		8 52			1123	1243			2 27		2 32 2 51			3 24	3 36		5 9

Week Days—Continued / Sundays

	aft	aft E	aft E	aft S	aft S	aft E	aft	aft		mrn	mrn		aft	aft
3 London (Liverpool St) ..dep	3 46	4 0	4 54	4 18	5 10	6 0		7 30		8 30	1150		4 0	6 8
Colchester...dep	5 8	6 0	6 24	6 20	6 40	7 27		9 20		1030	1 45		5 40	8 5
St. Botolph's arr		6 6		6 26			9 9							
St. Botolph's dep		6 14		6 31			9 9							
Hythe		6 18		6 35		7 32	9 13			1035	1 50			8 10
Wivenhoe arr	5 16	6 23	6 32	6 40	6 48	7 37	9 18	9 28		1040	1 55		5 49	8 15
Wivenhoe ...dep			6 38		6 53	7 43		9 33		1046	2 1		5 55	8 20
Brightlingsea arr			6 50		7 5	7 55		9 45		1058	2 13		6 7	8 32
Wivenhoe ...dep	5 18		6 34		6 49	7 39		9 29		1042	1 57		5 50	8 16
Alresford					6 55	7 45		9V35		1048	2 3			8 22
Thorington					6 59	7 49		9V39		1052	2 7			8 26
Great Bentley	5 28		6 44		7 3	7 53		9V43		1056	2 11			8 30
Weeley			6 50		7 8	7 58		9V48		11 1	2 16			8 35
Thorpe-le-Soken arr	5 38		6 55		7 12	8 2		9 52		11 5	2 20		6 48	8 39
Thorpe-le-Soken...dep	5 44		7 1		7 18	8 9		9 58		1112	2 26		6 12	8 46
Kirby Cross	5 50		7 7		7 24	8 15		10 4		1118	2 32		6 18	8 52
Frinton-on-Sea	5 54		7 12		7 29	8 20		10 8		1123	2 37		6 22	8 56
Walton-on-Naze arr	5 57		7 15		7 32	8 23		1011		1126	2 40		6 25	8 59
Thorpe-le-Soken...dep	5 40		6 57		7 14	8 5		9 54		11 8	2 22		6 8	8 42
Clacton-on-Sea A arr	5 49		7 6		7 25	8 14		10 3		1117	2 31		6 17	8 51

NOTES

A Clacton-on-Sea and Holland-on-Sea

E Except Saturdays

S Saturdays only

V Calls to set down only

COLCHESTER

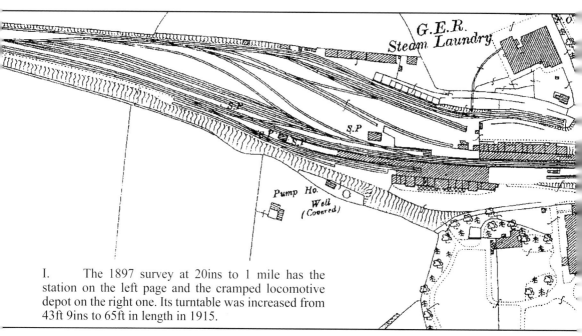

I.   The 1897 survey at 20ins to 1 mile has the station on the left page and the cramped locomotive depot on the right one. Its turntable was increased from 43ft 9ins to 65ft in length in 1915.

1.   The ECR terminus was in use as such for all trains for three years and is probably the hut on the map, west of the down platform and devoid of rails. The northern boundary fence indicates the alignment of the first railway. The EUR was built further south, resulting in the reverse curves seen on the left page. The up starting signals can be seen at the end of the roof. (P.Laming coll.)

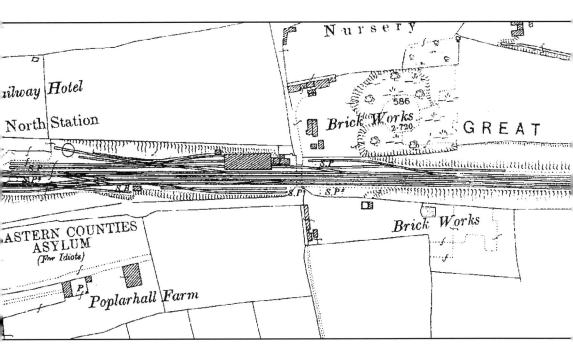

Nursery

ilway Hotel

North Station

586

Brick Works
2·720

GREAT

ASTERN COUNTIES
ASYLUM
(For Idiots)

P.

Poplarhall Farm

Brick Works

2.   The second station was lost when a new one was built on the site of the present one in 1865. Its down side is featured in this postcard view from around 1900, along with a recent GER 2-4-0. This type became LNER class E4. (P.Laming coll.)

3.　　At the west end of the station at about the same time is 2-4-0 class T19 no. 1037, plus a shunting horse. The short platform on the left was for horse traffic and a horse box stands on the right. In 1929, 18 private sidings were listed at Colchester, but most were east of the town. (P.Laming coll.)

4.　　The engine shed on the right page of the map was the second and was built in 1891. It was replaced by this three-road one in 1931, which was photographed on 19th October 1935. In front of the coaling plant is class D15 4-4-0 no. 8897. The depot closed on 2nd November 1959 and had often been congested with over 60 locomotives based here. (H.C.Casserley)

5.   The south elevation of the up side of the 1865 building is pictured in about 1950. Much of it still stood in 2011, but the main ticket office has been on the down side for about 50 years. (F.Ellersley coll.)

6.   We are witnessing the approach of "Britannia" class 4-6-2 no. 70003 *John Bunyan* on 14th March 1952, hauling the 10.30am Liverpool Street to Cromer. This class worked to Clacton from 1958. The signal box had 32 levers and was in use from 1888 until 1960. Its successor had a panel and lasted until December 1983. The goods yard closed on 18th April 1966, but much of it was subsequently used for other railway purposes. (B.I.Nathan)

7.   Class J15 0-6-0 no. 65424 waits in the bay with a Brightlingsea train on 9th August 1956. The map is self evident. The obsolete terminology on it is now in bad taste. (B.Pask)

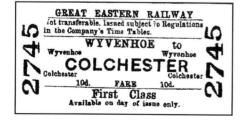

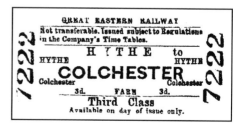

8.   From the same viewpoint, we see class B1 4-6-0 no. 61058 standing by the fogmans hut, with the first two coaches on the road bridge. On the left is evidence of the bay electrification and on the right is the chimney of the former GER laundry. The date is 24th May 1958. (F.Hornby)

9.   This is a down relief Clacton Express on 24th May 1958 and is seen behind class B17/6 4-6-0 no. 61612 *Houghton Hall*. The pair of cylinders on the smokebox are a reminder that trains from Liverpool Street retained the air brakes introduced by the GER. (F.Hornby)

10.   Turning round, we see class B12/3 4-6-0 no. 61553 bringing in empty stock to form the 2.01pm to Cambridge on 2nd October 1957. Largely hidden by steam is Colchester Junction signal box, which functioned from 1921 to 4th February 1962. It had 67 levers. A box was built in 1938, but never used and a workman was killed during its demolition in about 1960. (B.S.Jennings)

Other views can be found in the companion album *Shenfield to Ipswich*.

11.   Extensive rebuilding took place in 1959-62 and here we see the horse platform remaining, before completion of the down island platform. Platform 6 was created for Sudbury line trains, but by the 21st century was used only by London trains starting here in peak hours. (H.C.Casserley)

III.   The flyunder for the down Clacton route was completed in 1962 and this line was the only one on this diagram not to have bidirectional running east of the platforms, thereafter.

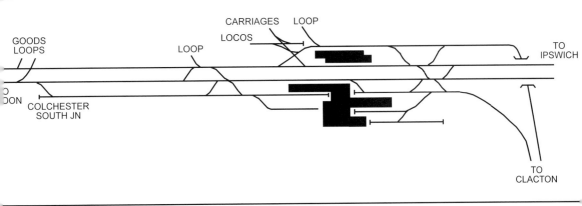

12.   An unusual feature was the creation of an inset platform which allowed an up stopping train from Clacton to London to wait while an express called to collect those passengers needing an earlier arrival. No. 309615 is leading on 11th May 1977. (B.Mills)

13.   Part of the former goods yard formed a locomotive depot and outside it on 31st January 1981 are nos 47115, 08228 and 08256. There were also five carriage sidings, two goods loops, two reception lines and eleven sidings for the engineers. The town grew from around 38,000 in 1900 to 100,000 in 2000 and there were 4.5m passengers in 2008. (F.Hornby)

14.   The signalling centre came into use in 1983 and its area of control gradually increased. In front of it on 18th June 2005 is no. 67014 and it is standing on one of the electrified loops. Sadly the station still does not have the suffix "North", despite widespread local use of it. (B.I.Nathan)

EAST OF COLCHESTER

IV.   The town is seen on the 1946 survey at 2ins to 1 mile. It had an electric street tramway in 1904-29. The main line is across the top and the branch curves from it. The 1962 down flyunder was built near this junction. The triangular junction has East Gate Junction at the top, Colne Junction on the left and Hythe Junction on the right, beyond which is Hythe station. St. Botolph's terminus is left of centre and the River Colne meanders from top left to lower right.

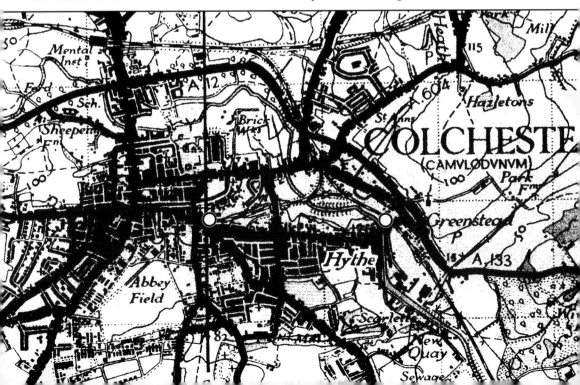

15.   A view south has the line to Clacton in the centre and the branch to St. Botolph's curving to the right. The box came into use on 1st December 1924 and it had 35 levers, plus a gate wheel. It also worked Colne Junction from 28th July 1925 after its 20-lever box of 1886 closed. The work of Hythe Junction box was transferred here on 7th December 1958. Its box also dated from 1886, but it had 38 levers. (A.Vaughan)

16.   We now have three photographs from 26th February 2009. Lifting barriers replaced the gates on 24th March 1974, with control being from the box. New signals came in December 1958 and the panel arrived in 1983. Lower right on the diagram is the flyunder line. Closure came on 17th April 2009. (D.C.Pearce)

17.	The two west side barriers and the staff crossing are seen from the points. The previous signal box had 30 levers and was completed in 1886, when the St. Botolph's line was doubled. The route between Colchester and Wivenhoe was also doubled in 1886. Great Bentley to Thorpe-le-Soken followed in 1890 and the section between was completed in 1898. (D.C.Pearce)

18.	The southward view from the signal box shows the severity of the curve and the speed restriction on it. No. 321311 has National Express East Anglia branding and is working the 14.45 Colchester Town to Colchester service. (D.C.Pearce)

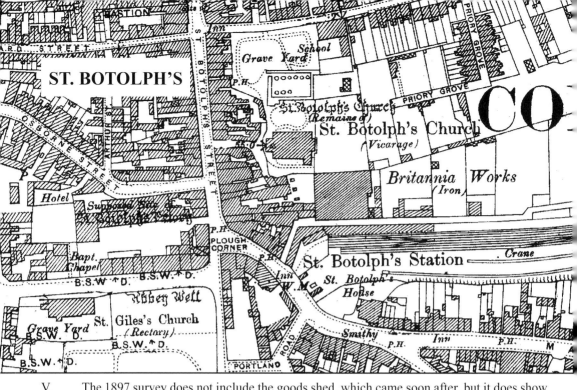

V. The 1897 survey does not include the goods shed, which came soon after, but it does show a theatre, which would have generated much passenger traffic. Railway horses would have kept the smithy busy.

19. Seen in 1911, the 41-lever box was in use from 1884 until 17th July 1983. It controlled Paxman's siding and a stabling siding until November 1971. (D.Brennand coll.)

20.   Viewed from the same footbridge about ten years later is the goods yard, with its original small crane. On the right is the church after which the station was named. (F.Ellersley coll.)

21.   The end of the line is seen in about the same period, when most road transport was horse drawn and lighting was by gas. The town had its own power station in 1927. (F.Ellersley coll.)

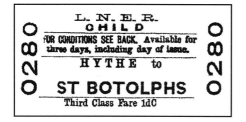

L. N. E. R.
CHILD
FOR CONDITIONS SEE BACK. Available for three days, including day of issue.
HYTHE   to
ST BOTOLPHS
Third Class Fare 1d 0
0280 0280

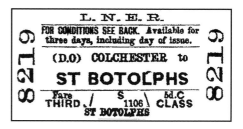

L. N. E. R.
FOR CONDITIONS SEE BACK. Available for three days, including day of issue.
(D.O) COLCHESTER to
ST BOTOLPHS
Fare   /   S   5d.C
THIRD   1106   CLASS
ST BOTOLPHS
8219 8219

22.　　A final postcard completes our survey of this important goods yard. The connections to part of it were removed in November 1976. Total closure came on the 7th June 1982. (P.Laming coll.)

23.　　The house for the station master is on the left and attached to it are the station offices. One would be for parcels and the solitary van was probably involved with that traffic. This part of the town was very industrialised. The view is from 1950. (F.Ellersley coll.)

24.   The public footbridge from which pictures 19 and 20 were taken now comes into view, along with the sidings in the cutting. This had been widened since the production of map V. (F.Ellersley coll.)

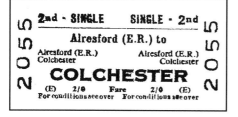

25.   Class B17/1 4-6-0 no. 61611 *Raynham Hall* is running round the 6.35pm Clacton to Colchester stopping train on 17th April 1949. Trains from Brightlingsea often terminated or reversed here, as the station is so convenient for the town centre. (W.A.Camwell/SLS coll.)

26.   Included in this view are the extensive sidings east of the station, together with the footbridge. Only the nearest one was electrified. (Norfolk Railway Society)

27.   The masts and wires are up for the AC trial scheme as class N7/3 0-6-2T no. 69732 waits to depart in August 1958. The crane capacity had been increased to 6-tons. (B.Pask)

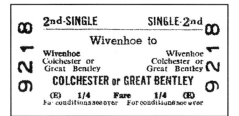

28.   A DMU waits to depart for Brightlingsea on 1st June 1963, complete with cats whiskers. It was possible to see diesel, electric and steam traction on the route in 1959-64. (R.B.Parr/D.Brennand coll.)

29.   The area of grass had carried the loop line until June 1983. No. 312729 is working the 12.26 Colchester to Clacton on 6th August 1988. The platform could take 12 coaches. The flags are out for the second anniversary of the formation of NSE, when cheap touring tickets were available. The event was actually eight weeks late, but the £1 Explorer tickets were worth waiting for. (Dr. I.C.Scotchman)

COLCHESTER TOWN

30.   The name was changed on 15th July 1991, although St. Botolph's Church is still adjacent.
No. 312703 is in NSE colours, as it waits to reverse on 4th October 1991.
(P.Hurst/Colour-Rail.com)

→ VI. Hythe Junction and its signal box are top left on this 1930s map. The first railway reached the east bank of the Colne on 1st April 1847, but confirmation of a passenger service on it has not been found, despite local newspapers having been searched on line. The bridge and tramway to the west bank date from about 1852, but the tramway closed during 1870-79. It was extended south of the wharf in 1884 and reached the coal yard of the gas works in 1917. Extension to its south yard took place in 1926. The line was worked by a tram engine until a Drewry diesel arrived. Finally, a Fordson tractor was used. The quays were still busy in 1965, with 2000 vessels averaging 250 tons arriving. Two sidings of the goods yard were still in place in 2011, these having served a coal concentration depot. Colchester Gas Company opened on this site in 1839, having had three previous premises. It received almost all its coal by sea, except during World War II. Coke and other by-products left by rail. From the mid-1960s oil was used instead of coal and closure came in 1971.

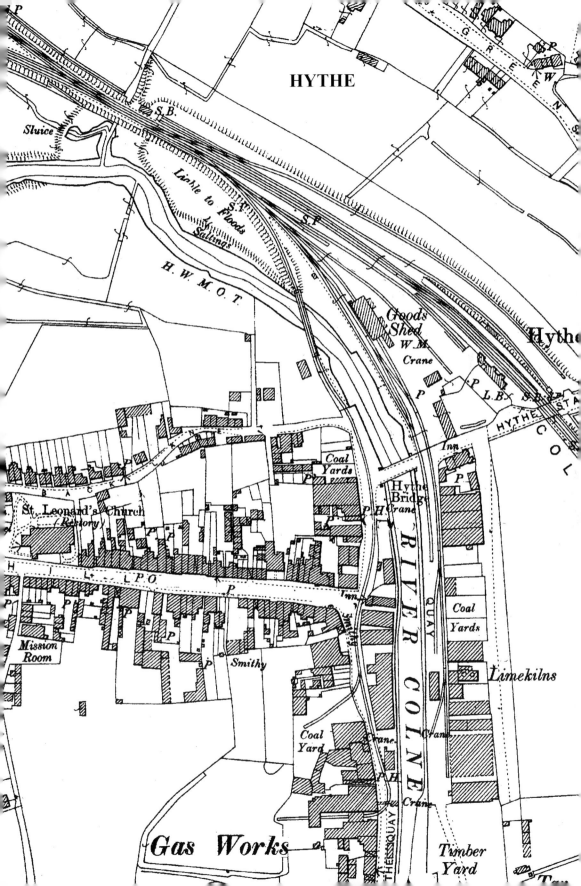

HYTHE

Sluice

S.B.

Liable to Floods

Saltings

H. W. M. O. T.

Goods Shed

W. M. Crane

Hythe

P

P L.B. S.B.

HYTHE COL

Inn

Coal Yards

P

Hythe Bridge

P H Crane

St. Leonard's Church
(Rectory)

H I L L P O

P

Inn

Smithy

QUAY

RIVER COLNE

Coal Yards

Limekilns

Mission Room

Smithy

Coal Yard

Crane

P H

Crane

Crane

Gas Works

THE QUAY

Timber Yard

Tan

31.   The gates were moved by hand and there was a lever in the hut to lock them. The later lifting barriers were controlled from East Gate junction box. (P.Laming coll.)

32.   The first two locomotives for the Romney Hythe & Dymchurch Railway were built here by Davey Paxman in 1925. No. 1 *Green Goddess* has been loaded for conveyance to the Ravenglass & Eskdale Railway, for testing. Its off-centre position suggests that no. 2 *Northern Chief* is about to follow alongside. See *Romneyrail* (Middleton Press) for 120 more photographs. (RH&DR coll.)

33.   The up side was recorded on 7th July 1956. Both platforms were later cleared to accommodate a bus shelter each. The goods yard once had a 15-ton crane, but was closed on 31st January 1966. It continued to be used for coal for many years. Finally it was used for Redland's stone traffic, their last train being on 8th April 1995. (H.C.Casserley)

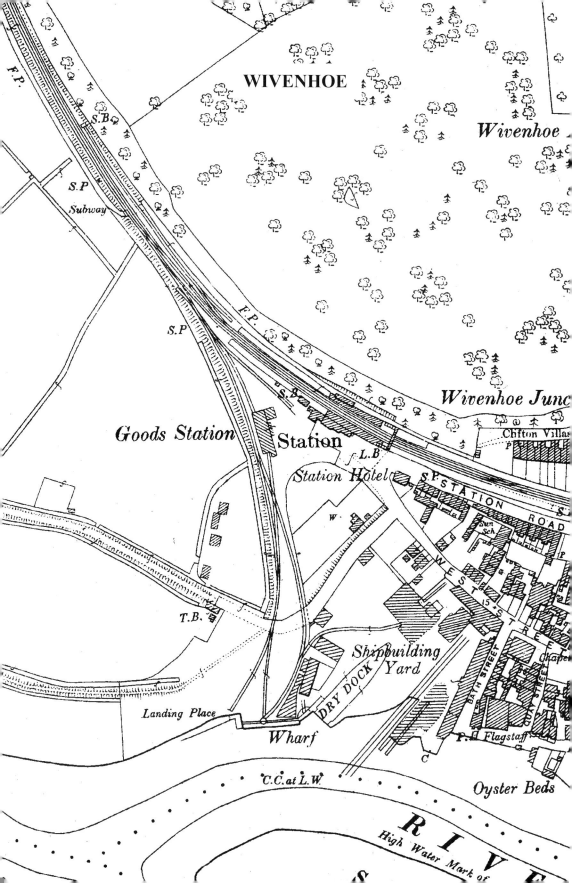

WIVENHOE

Wivenhoe

F.P.

S.B.

S.P

Subway

S.P

F.P.

S.B.

Wivenhoe Junc

Clifton Villa

Goods Station

Station

L.B

Station Hotel

S.P STATION

ROAD

Sun Sch.

w

WEST ST

15 ST

T.B.

Shipbuilding Yard

DRY DOCK

BATH STREET

QUAY STREET

Chapel

Landing Place

Wharf

P. Flagstaff

C

Oyster Beds

C.C. at L.W

R I V E

High Water Mark of

The Nook

P.H)

Almshouses

REBOW ROAD

School

MALTING YARD

P.O.

QUEENS ROAD

School

PAGET ROAD

Colne Villa
Elaine Cottage

Union Bdy.

VII.   The 1897 map was produced one year
before a junction was created near the right
border at the time of the doubling of the route
eastwards. The lower line is to Brightlingsea
and it always remained single. The GER used
the spelling WYVENHOE from July 1879 until
October 1911, but the cartographers did not.
There was a bay for Brightlingsea trains until
1886; it was above STATION of Station Road.
The town undertook shipbuilding from 1588
until 1944.

St. Mary's
Church

FALCON YD

ALMA STREET

Grave Yard

EAST STREET

BROAD STREET

Spring

B.H.

PAGET ROAD

Yachtsman's Arms
(P.H.)

F.B.

C.D.

THE QUAY

BETHANY

ST JOHNS ROAD

Gas
Works

Liable to Flood

THE FOLLY

F.P.

Ferry

Flagstaff

Shipbuilding

34.　　A postcard view towards Clacton includes the 1886 signal box, which had 31 levers. It remained in use until 23rd July 1967. The pole on the left carries wires in three directions. (P.Laming coll.)

35.　　We look east at Wivenhoe Junction box, which contained 20 levers and functioned from 1st July 1898 to 17th July 1938. The tide is high around the Brightlingsea branch. (P.Laming coll.)

36.   An westward panorama from the High Street includes co-acting signals of value where bridges occluded views. Station Road is in front of the houses on the left. (P.Laming coll.)

37.   The full name is evident as class J15 0-6-0 no. 65448 runs in at 5.45pm on 17th April 1949, with a train for Brightlingsea. The population reached 3300 in 1961. (W.A.Camwell/SLS coll.)

38. The south elevation of the goods shed is to be seen on the left, as class J15 0-6-0 no. 65456 faces the wharf in 1954. The nearby large sheds were used for shipbuilding until 1944. The goods yard closed on 4th October 1965. (F.Ellersley coll.)

39. High Street bridge is in the distance as ex-LTSR class 3P 4-4-2T no. 41949 waits to depart for Clacton in March 1954. The symbolism of having a lavatory window in the shape of a lavatory seat has always impressed your pencil pusher. (H.C.Casserley)

40.   The buildings have changed little since being photographed in the 1980s. The population had been only 2193 in 1931. (B.Pask)

41.   Many canopies were cut back in 1959 to improve clearance for the AC wires. NSE paintwork seemed to suit class 312 EMUs and this one is about to make easy work of the climb eastwards, some of which is at 1 in 71. (B.Pask)

NORTH OF BRIGHTLINGSEA

42.   Alresford Creek was navigable when the branch opened and so a ten-span 462ft long iron bridge was built, with a hand cranked swing span. Its bearing when open is on the left. There were signals until 1927, when a bridgemans hut was provided and electrical interlocking came in. The branch embankments were severely damaged by flood waters on 1st February 1953 and the line did not reopen until 7th December of that year. (Dr. G.B.Sutton)

43.   There were three wooden trestle bridges nearer Brightlingsea and one is seen under repair prior to 1923. Their lengths were 670ft, 247ft and 328ft from north to south. (F.Ellersley coll.)

BRIGHTLINGSEA

VIII. The 1895 edition emphasises the importance of oyster production and shows that two tracks were roofed over. The number of residents rose from 3075 in 1871 to 4950 in 1961. Lower left is a ballast siding used during line construction, but it subsequently remained disconnected.

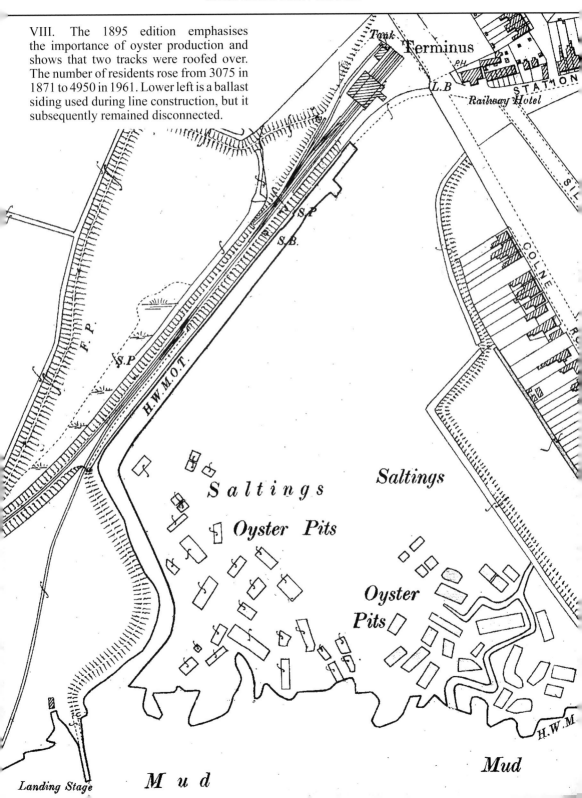

Tank

Terminus

P.H.

L.B

STATION

Railway Hotel

COLNE RO...

SIL...

S.P.

S.B.

F.P.

S.P.

H.W.M.O.T.

Saltings

Saltings

Oyster Pits

Oyster Pits

H.W.M.

Landing Stage

M u d

Mud

44.   The original wooden station apparently acted as a wind tunnel and there was rejoicing when it burnt down on 31st December 1901. This postcard shows the 1906 replacement, plus the engine shed to the right of it. (F.Ellersley coll.)

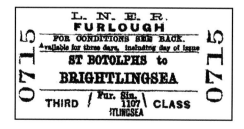

45.　　The new station was included on a postcard, but the signal box of the same date was not. It had 22 levers and was replaced in 1922 by a 3-lever ground frame. Traffic figures for 1932 were: tickets issued 372,705, coal received 5827 tons and general merchandise 1893 tons. (P.Laming coll.)

46.　　The barrels were used for the conveyance of oysters and sprats in vast quantities. Much of the traffic went to Parkeston Quay for export to mainland Europe. The white patches are on a cattle truck, these being due to lime used as an antiseptic. (P.Laming coll.)

47.   The single road engine shed (left) was added in 1901 and it normally housed one 2-4-2T. It was closed in 1939 and was subsequently used for a permanent way trolley . The coaches on the left are on the line to the goods shed. On the right is class F3 2-4-2T no. 8041 on 28th March 1937. (W.A.Camwell/SLS coll.)

48.   The run-round loop was extended in 1937 and has just been used by class J15 0-6-0 no. 65432 on 7th July 1956. Compartment stock stands at the platform. Bank holiday trains in the late 1940s would sometimes exceed the platform length. (H.C.Casserley)

↓ 49. DMUs replaced steam on the branch on 4th March 1957 and diesels took over freight tasks in May 1960. The very severe snow and ice early in 1963 caused serious delays and ruined the oyster trade. The 11.07am departure is seen on 2nd October 1957. All traffic ceased on 15th June 1964. (B.Jennings)

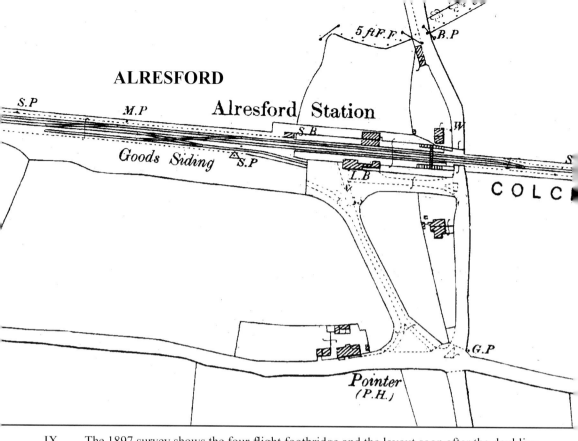

IX.   The 1897 survey shows the four-flight footbridge and the layout soon after the doubling.

50.   The architectural style chosen by the THR can be enjoyed here and further east. The staff had much spare time to attend to floral matters. (F.Ellersley coll.)

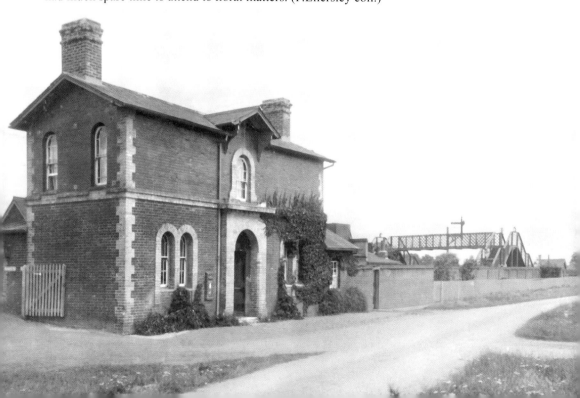

51. A generous canopy arrived on the down side after the doubling, but most trains did not stop here in the first half of the 20th century. (F.Ellersley coll.)

52. The north elevation was recorded on 7th July 1956, when there were up departures am at 6.54, 7.45, 10.01, 10.52 and pm at 12.0l, 2.57, 4.58, 6.44 and 9.24, on weekdays. There were three on Sundays. Most of the building was still standing in 2011. (H.C.Casserley)

53.   The signal box had 24 levers and was worked from 1889 until 21st December 1958. Behind the hedge is the goods yard, which was in use until 7th September 1964. Class J15 0-6-0 no. 65424 is passing through Alresford with Colchester breakdown vans on 17th August 1957. (B.Pask)

54.   It is 24th June 1984 and it is evident that the trial electrification scheme allowed retention of the complex lattice footbridge, but that the canopy required minor surgery. A modern shelter appeared later to replace the one seen. (B.W.L.Brooksbank)

THORINGTON

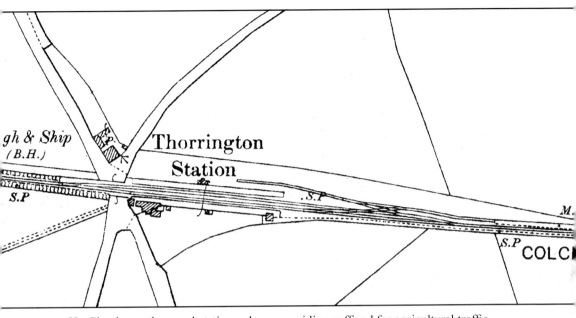

X. Clearly another rural station, where one siding sufficed for agricultural traffic.
The year is 1897.

55.   The lack of any up side weather protection is notable. The signal box was completed in 1885 and its 20-lever frame was used until 21st December 1958. (P.Laming coll.)

56.   BR class 4 2-6-0 no. 76031 is arriving on 17th August 1957. Passenger service ceased here on 4th November of that year and freight ended on 13th February 1961. (B.Pask)

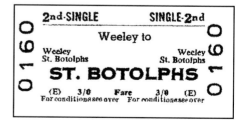

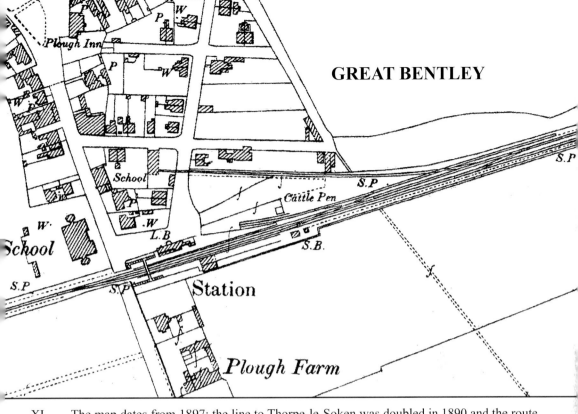

GREAT BENTLEY

XI.   The map dates from 1897; the line to Thorpe-le-Soken was doubled in 1890 and the route west of Great Bentley followed in 1898. There is a private siding shown which was for Charles Simmons, a coal merchant.

57.   Round head windows again adorn the scene and there is the extravagance of four flights of steps to the footbridge. The station was called Bentley Green until 1st May 1887. (P.Laming coll.)

58.   In the distance is the gate box, which remained in use until 28th May 1983. The nearest part of the main building is devoid of a roof and was for the benefit of gentlemen.
(F.Ellersley coll.)

→ 59. A down stopping train was recorded on 17th August 1957. In the background is the goods yard, which closed on 1st May 1967. Also visible is the signal box, which lasted until 21st December 1958. It was built in 1889 and a 30-lever frame was fitted in 1898.
(B.Pask)

→   60. Class B17/1 4-6-0 no. 61601 speeds through with a down express on 17th August 1957. The gatemans hut is on the right. The nearer part of the crossing was for barrows.
(B.Pask)

61.   The annual weed control train was photographed at 12.34 on 13th October 2007. (Dr. I.C.Scotchman)

62.   Seen on the same day is no. 321358 departing west, as the gateman closes the gates again. The bridge had been provided with a new span to give clearance for the wiring, but little else was altered. (Dr. I.C.Scotchman)

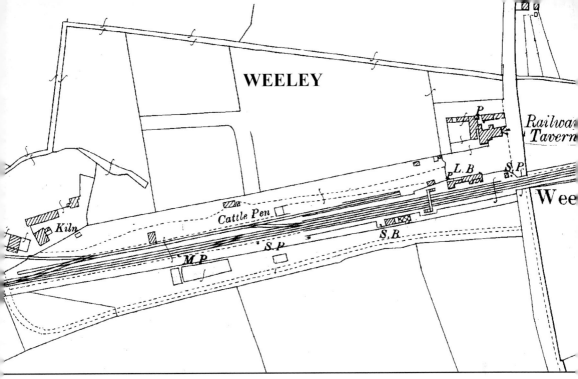

WEELEY

Kiln

Cattle Pen

M.P.

S.P.

S.B.

P

L.B.

S.P.

Railwa
Tavern

Wee

XII.   The 1897 issue includes a private siding for coal inwards and bricks outwards. British Petroleum had a siding from October 1928 and there were two more by 1938.

63.   A down train waits and the staff pose for a postcard photographer, early in the 20th century. The train appears to be composed of six-wheelers. (P.Laming coll.)

64.   A closer look at the main building reveals THR features. The low chimney (left) would have been subjected to major downdraught problems. (P.Laming coll.)

65.   The signal box is on the left in this 1950s view. Its 20-lever frame was used from 1884 until 21st December 1958. The goods yard is centre; it closed on 7th December 1964. (F.Ellersley coll.)

66.   A 1960s view towards Clacton shows that a new concrete bridge was erected prior to electrification. The old lamp room remains on the left. (Lens of Sutton coll.)

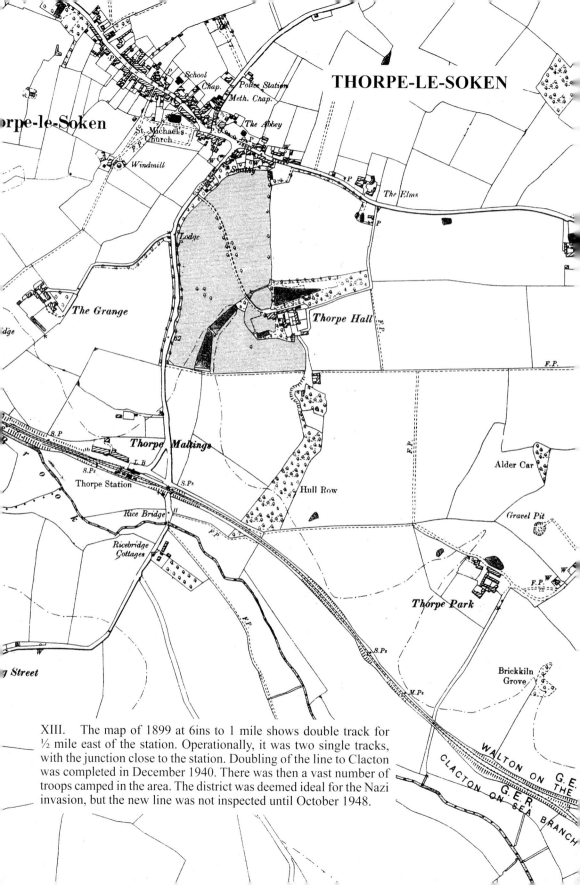

THORPE-LE-SOKEN

School
Chap.
Police Station
Meth. Chap.

orpe-le-Soken

The Abbey

St. Michael's
Church

Windmill

The Elms

Lodge

The Grange

52

Thorpe Hall

F.P.

F.P.

S.P.

Thorpe Maltings

L.B.

Alder Car

S.Ps

Thorpe Station

S.Ps

Rice Bridge

Hull Row

F.P.

Gravel Pit

Ricebridge
Cottages

Thorpe Park

F.P. W W

F.P.

Brickkiln
Grove

g Street

W

S.Ps

M.Ps

WALTON ON G.E.
THE

CLACTON ON SEA BRANCH

CLACTON ON G.E.R.

XIII.   The map of 1899 at 6ins to 1 mile shows double track for
½ mile east of the station. Operationally, it was two single tracks,
with the junction close to the station. Doubling of the line to Clacton
was completed in December 1940. There was then a vast number of
troops camped in the area. The district was deemed ideal for the Nazi
invasion, but the new line was not inspected until October 1948.

67.   The main buildings were on the north side of the line and beyond them are the maltings. The suffix "-le-Soken" was added in July 1900 and the population was 1065 in 1901. It grew to 1606 by 1961. There are notices in the shadows on the canopy on the right for the benefit of agricultural developers and gardeners as well as soldiers. (F.Ellersley coll.)

68.   Class F5 2-4-2T no. 67188 is nearest, while a class J68 0-6-0 creeps in on the right. The building was dedicated to gentlemen and was demolished as part of the electrification works. (F.Ellersley coll.)

69.   Featured centre is class B17/1 4-6-0 no. 61644 *Earlham Hall* with a train from Clacton on 17th April 1949. On the right are the coaches from Walton, which will be shunted onto the back of it. (W.A.Camwell/SLS coll.)

XIV. Signalling diagram for 1950. TC indicates Track Circuit.

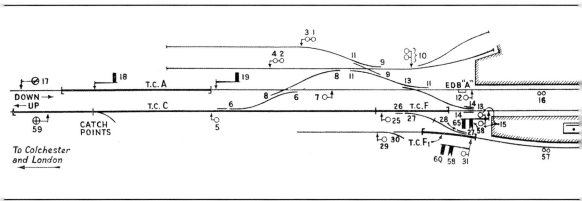

70.   A different procedure is in progress on 13th August 1957, as the portion from Walton is being attached to the front of the Clacton coaches. GER could still be found under the platform seats. (B.Pask)

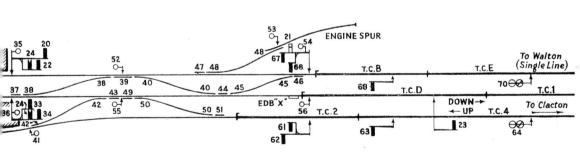

71.   Seen on the same day is class B1 4-6-0 no. 61280. This class was introduced in 1942, but only a few carried names. The small goods yard is on the right; it was closed on 1st May 1967. (B.Pask)

72.   The final picture from that day features class B17/1 4-6-0 no. 61600 *Sandringham* leaving the station, with a down train for Clacton. (B.Pask)

73.   It is late 1950s, when steam and electric traction overlapped. Class N7/3 0-6-2T no. 69713 pilots class J15 0-6-0 no. 65441 on a down train for Clacton. The colour light signals are not yet in use. (F.Ellersley coll.)

74.   Class 15 no. D8225 represents the diesel era in this view from the same period. A local down train is on the far side and a new footbridge has arrived. Albrew Maltsters' building became listed, but was allowed to decay to a ruin before wall stabilisation started in 2011. (F.Ellersley coll.)

75.   The arrangement was recorded on 22nd May 1971, looking east. A new ticket office was erected at the foot of the steps and the track on the left was lifted later. (R.F.Roberts/SLS coll.)

76.   The north elevation is pictured, the view being from August 1984. There were no single-line tokens to Kirby Cross, but an unusual direction lever which employed a "sweeping relay" was employed instead. (R.M.Rickard/Colour-Rail.com)

77.　　This panel was fitted into the 1882 signal box in July 1989, it replacing a 70-lever frame. There was one with 50 levers until 1937, when control was extended to Kirby Cross. Walton is top right on the diagram, which is seen on 1st May 2009. Colchester took over the next day. (D.A.Pollock)

78.　　Seen from the footbridge, the new ticket office and waiting room is lower right in this panorama from 20th September 2008. The down platform was fenced off, not having been used regularly since May 1982. (B.W.L.Brooksbank)

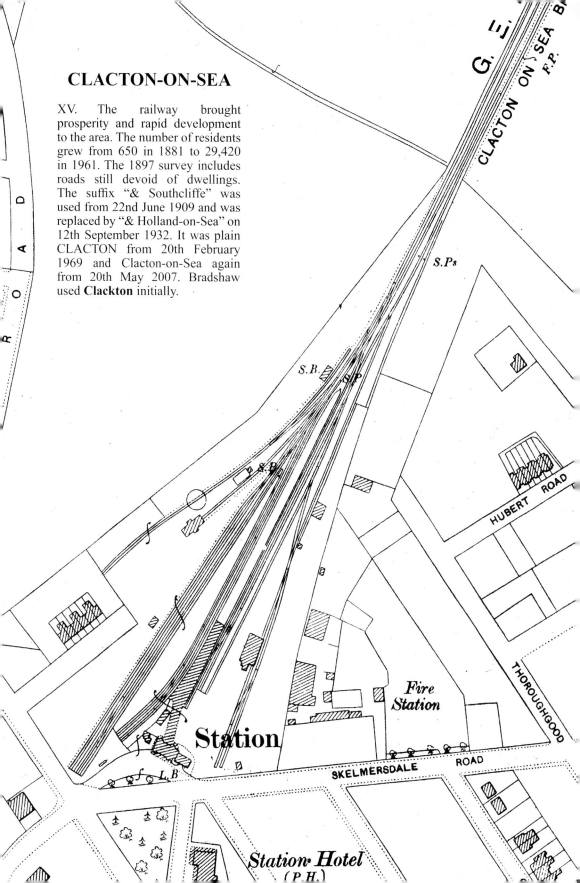

CLACTON-ON-SEA

XV. The railway brought prosperity and rapid development to the area. The number of residents grew from 650 in 1881 to 29,420 in 1961. The 1897 survey includes roads still devoid of dwellings. The suffix "& Southcliffe" was used from 22nd June 1909 and was replaced by "& Holland-on-Sea" on 12th September 1932. It was plain CLACTON from 20th February 1969 and Clacton-on-Sea again from 20th May 2007. Bradshaw used **Clackton** initially.

G. E. \[\]

CLACTON ON SEA B

F.P.

S.Ps

S.B.

S.P

P. S. B.

ROAD

HUBERT ROAD

THOROUGHGOOD

Station

Fire Station

L.B.

SKELMERSDALE ROAD

Station Hotel (P.H.)

79.	The well proportioned terminal building was on an early postcard, along with an omnibus of the 1910-15 era. The chimneys were of brick, but the remainder was of timber. (F.Ellersley coll.)

80.	Platforms 1 and 2 are featured, along with the goods shed, which housed a 30cwt crane. There were seven private sidings listed in 1938. (F.Ellersley coll.)

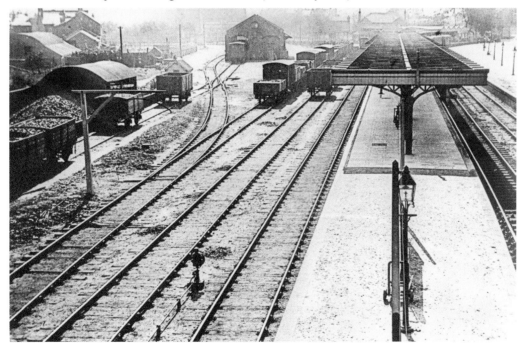

81.   The single road engine shed housed one locomotive from the opening of the line, but blew down in the mid-1920s. The turntable (right) was 45ft 6ins in length and was replaced by one of 60ft in 1927. The replacement was built near the G of GER on the map and is shown in picture 83. (BR)

82.   Rebuilding took place between December 1928 and November 1929. Traffic was growing immensely and so a spacious concourse was created. (F.Ellersley coll.)

83.   This two-road engine shed was completed in 1929 and usually had five locomotives in the 1930s. There were seven B17s and one J69 in 1954. It closed to steam on 13th April 1959. (W.A.Camwell/SLS)

84.   Two platforms on the right were provided initially and the two on the left arrived in July 1891. This was because of increasing excursion traffic and they are seen in 1930. (F.Ellersley coll.)

85.   The signal box was built in 1891 and its 52 levers were increased to 64 in 1930. The number was 69 from 1940, in readiness for the doubling to Thorpe-le-Soken. Picture 80 was taken from the signal post right of centre. (F.Ellersley coll.)

86.   Seen from platform 2 on 7th July 1956 is class B17/1 4-6-0 no. 61606 *Audley End*, heading the 6.0pm to Liverpool Street. (H.C.Casserley)

87.   A subject of limited cleaning, class B17/4 4-6-0 no. 61663 *Everton* is under observation by serious railway students in the 1950s. Your author stood in a similar position in August 1944 and was distinctly impressed by the 8.15am departure, as it was hauled by a B17, but had only one coach of the type seen in picture 24. Few folk had returned to Clacton by that part of the war. (F.Ellersley coll.)

↓ 88. The concourse was photographed in the late 1950s, when around 140,000 tickets were issued per annum and 700,000 collected. (F.Ellersley coll.)

89.   The goods yard (right) closed on 2nd October 1964. The view is from platform 3, with no. 2 on the right. This is shortly before the signalling was upgraded to colour light on the 8th February 1959. The signal box avoided threatened closure in April 2009. (F.Ellersley coll.)

90.   Class 24 diesel no. D5046 is departing on 22nd April 1961. The footbridge was built near the diagonal fences top right on the map. On the right is the then new carriage washing plant. (F.Ellersley coll.)

91.   The engine shed seen in picture 83 was extended in asbestos to form a workshop for EMUs and the wooden part was demolished later. (F.Ellersley coll.)

92.   Standing at platform 2 in August 1986 is EMU no. 308136. Platforms 1 and 3 will take eight coaches and the other two accommodate 12. (A.C.Mott)

93.   The main entrance is seen deserted in 1986, but on Saturdays in the Summers of the 1950s up to 10,000 people could be queuing along the road, after a day on the beach. (A.C.Mott)

94.   A traction maintenance depot was opened on 17th July 1981, but closed in January 1994, when the class 309s were withdrawn. Berthing sidings were retained and the depot was reopened by Siemens in 2003 for maintaining class 360 units. No. 360110 is seen on 26th February 2003 in one of the five sidings. (Dr. I.C.Scotchman)

JAYWICK MINIATURE RAILWAY

95.   Jaywick Sands had become a popular holiday location in the 1920s and the Tudor Village Estate was begun ½ mile inland in the mid-1930s. Its office is in the background and their prices began at £325 for a two-bedroomed dwelling. An 18 ins-gauge railway was built by the developers to overcome the problem of the remoteness of the beach and the train ran at 30-minute intervals. This is the inland terminus, which was called Crossways and the engine shed was located here. It housed no. 1, which was a one-third model of a GNR Stirling Single, which had been obtained by the Fairbourne Railway in 1926 (see Middleton Press album *Machynlleth to Barmouth*). It had been built from parts made by Bagnall in 1897 and it ran to Jaywick from the line's opening on 31st July 1936, until the Autumn of 1938. After many moves, it entered the 21st century as an exhibit in a museum at Littleham, in South Devon. (NGRS News 168)

A 4021

JAYWICK MINIATURE RAILWAY.

The Miniature Railway & Specialists Engineering Co. 127/131, Terminus Road, Eastbourne.

SINGLE
Or Non-Stop Return

4d

PUNCH & TICKET CO. LONDON, N1

96.   No. 1 is seen at the terminus at Jaywick Sands in 1936. Most of the route was built on the top of a flood defence bank and so there were extensive vistas. The three coaches seated 24 each and were built by Caffyns of Eastbourne, a firm that was still in the motor trade in that town in 2011. The coaches were painted SR green and were fitted with air brakes. (NGRS News 168)

97.   No. 2 was built for the line by Sentinel and it had a vertical water-tube boiler, which used liquid fuel (TVO) and could raise steam in eight minutes. The line closed in September 1939, due to the advent of World War II and the stock was dispersed in 1946, although much of it survived. The southern half of the route was reopened in 1949, but without loops. A 1936 Orenstein & Koppel diesel locomotive was regauged from 2ft to 18ins, but it ran for that Summer only and there is now no trace of this unusual railway. (NGRS News 168)

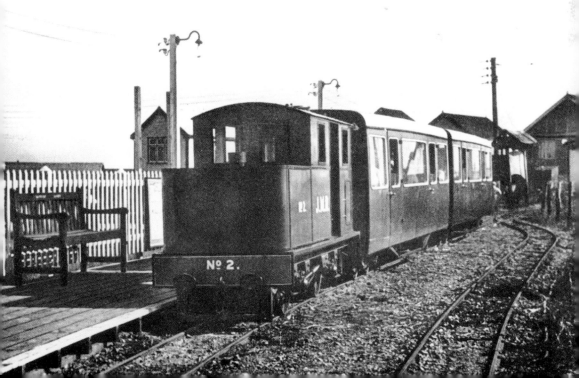

KIRBY CROSS

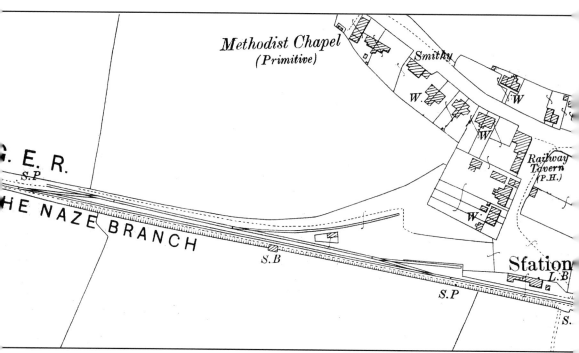

XVI.   The 1897 survey includes a goods loop. A passing loop and up platform were provided in October 1899. Goods traffic ceased here on 31st July 1961.

98.   Another well composed postcard includes the 26-lever signal box, which was functional from 1899 to 31st October 1990. The hoop carried the single line tablet. (P.Laming coll.)

99.   The detail of the paraffin lamp can be seen as we watch class N7/3 0-6-2T no. 69727 entering Kirby Cross with a train from Walton on 13th August 1957. Note that the signal post is a perforated concrete one of LNER design. (B.Pask)

100.   With the much admired curved windows, a class 309 EMU forms the 11.30 Colchester to Walton on 31st October 1973. There was a siding east of the station for the Tendring Hundred Water Company and also the gas works from 1928 until about 1948. (R.F.Roberts/SLS coll.)

101.   In NSE livery, no. 321308 is working the 14.40 Walton-on-Naze to Thorpe-le-Soken service on 7th December 1989. The crossing in the foreground was for use by passengers and also was a public right of way. (D.A.Pollock)

102.   Although the building was boarded up when photographed on 20th September 2008, both platforms were still in use, accommodating eight coaches each. (B.W.L.Brooksbank)

FRINTON-ON-SEA

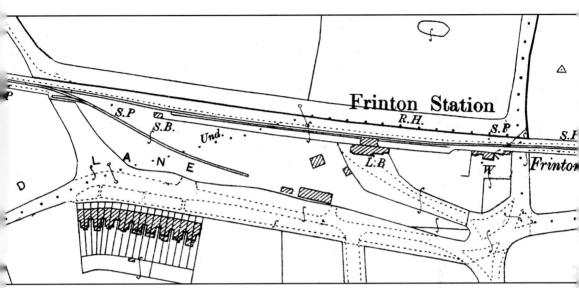

XVII. The station was Frinton for its first two months, Frinton-on-Sea until 20th February 1969, plain Frinton until 20th May 2007 and Frinton-on-Sea again subsequently. The first Wireless Telegraph School in the world was established here in 1901 by Marconi, but was transferred to Chelmsford in 1904.

103. The official opening date was 1st July 1888 and a 16-lever signal box was in use (behind the camera) from 8th June 1888 until 31st October 1922. The down platform and loop were opened on 6th October 1937. (F.Ellersley coll.)

104.   The rural position was depicted on a postcard. The route to Walton was built close to the beach and was subjected to much erosion. In 1929, it was resited inland, this involving the creation of a long cutting and a road bridge. (P.Laming coll.)

105.   This was the "Entrance to Frinton-on-Sea" of which it was proud. The signal box shows partially on the right; it was destroyed during bombing on 14th March 1943, but rebuilt by June. (P.Laming coll.)

106.   The gatekeepers house is included in this undated view of the north elevation of the signal box. The population increased from 644 in 1901 to 9900 in 1961. (F.Ellersley coll.)

107.　A 15-lever frame was fitted in 1937 and the box had to be enlarged. It was down graded to a gate box in 1974. (F.Ellersley coll.)

➜ 108.　The down line and platform were closed on 14th February 1959. The fire brigade's hose drying tower is in the background as class N7/3 0-6-2T no. 69721 runs in with an up train on 13th August 1957. (B.Pask)

➜　109.　The reduction of the up canopy width presented problems here, as it was made of ferro-concrete and a thermic lance had to be used. The shelter on the left was still standing in 2011 and had been lined with murals. Class N7/3 no. 69708 is westbound on a busy Saturday in early 1959. (Dr. G.B.Sutton)

110.   The replacement of the level crossing gates by barriers led to local uproar and questions in Parliament. The battle was lost on 17th April 2009. The pill box (left) was kept in case of an invasion. A ban on public houses had ended in 2000. Earlier attempts to perpetuate civilisation had resulted in the LNER's famous poster "HARWICH for the CONTINENT" being once defaced to show "FRINTON for the INCONTINENT". (D.A.Pollock)

WALTON-ON-THE-NAZE

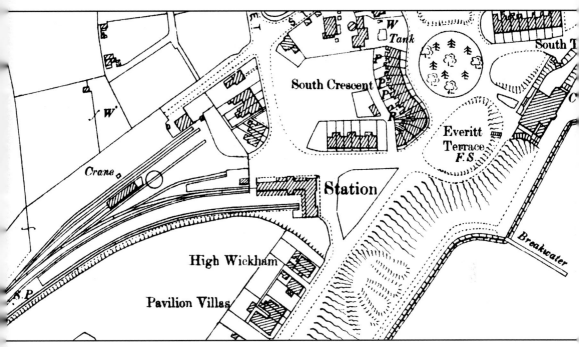

XVIII. The use of "the" in the name has varied over the years, but since 8th May 2007 it has been in use on the station again, although most in the town had kept it. The crane shown was rated at 2-tons.

111.   The terminal building was L-shaped, as shown on the map, but not clear here. On the left is the small goods shed, which was not connected to the other structures. The camera is on the dock, otherwise known as the horse landing, as the gentry could have their horse & carriage unloaded here. (P.Laming coll.)

112.   Unlike Clacton pier, Walton's had a railway. A 3ft 6ins gauge electric line was laid in 1898. It had two cars, plus a spare, as seen. It was replaced in 1935 with one with pneumatic tyres running within wooden beams and powered by batteries. Following closure during World War II, a 2ft gauge line was laid to facilitate repairs to the pier. It was retained with a diesel locomotive, plus accommodation for passengers, until the 1970s. (Middleton Press coll.)

113.   The signalman's view shows six-wheeled coaches in one of the two berthing sidings, the engine shed centre and platform 2 on the right. The population grew from 697 in 1861 to 9900 in 1961. (F.Ellersley coll.)

↑ 114.   Class K1 2-6-0 no. 62067 departs on 13th August 1957, with the platform 1 signal still off. The signal box was probably the original one and had 28 levers for most of its life. (B.Pask)

115.   No. 65445 was a class J15 0-6-0, one of a type introduced in 1883. It is on station pilot duties on 6th April 1957. The shelter was built in about 1930. (D.Brennand coll.)

➜ 116.   Two locomotives were the common allocation at this shed, until closure came sometime in 1960. Nearest is class N7/3 0-6-2T no. 69730. Initially, the water quality and supply was so poor that it was brought from Weeley in a tanker. Out of view in the background was a 55ft long turntable. It replaced a 45ft 6ins one in 1938. (A.Morris/Colour-Rail.com)

➜ 117.   The east elevation was photographed on 23rd October 1989. The entire structure avoided demolition, only the small goods shed being lost. A new ticket office was built on its site. (P.Hurst/Colour-Rail com.)

118. The goods yard closed on 7th December 1964, but most of the sidings remained until October 1966. The signal box was in use until 10th October 1982, as were the two remaining sidings. (F.Ellersley coll.)

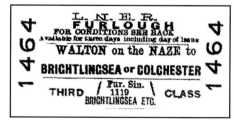

The Bottom Line

My grandparents were evacuated from their home in Clacton due to the threat of invasion, but were able to return after D-Day. My first rail visit soon followed, but having only experienced green compartment stock, I was astonished to find unpainted coaches with corridors. For this child, an even greater surprise was a device marked VACANT/ENGAGED. On arrival at our boarding house, I was delighted to find a replica, but it was so worn that I found that I could operate it from the outside, with one finger on the T.

Locking it upon leaving the room, I deemed that it would always be available for family use, but I forgot to tell my parents. I was almost asleep when I heard my enraged Father moaning that the toilet was always in use. "No trouble, Dad. I can open it" I said. You can imagine the row that followed.

However, it led to my fascination with sanitary engineering. While one famous artist always had a certain mouse in all his railway paintings, my interest has appeared in at least one caption in every album I have compiled since. Some have spotted it, but now they know why!

119.   Platform 2 was beyond the right border of the picture and was taken out of use on 17th May 1982. No. 312710 waits to leave for Thorpe-le-Soken at 14.08 on 6th August 1988. (Dr.I.C.Scotchman)

120.   The shelter seen in pictures 115 and 119 was still standing when the 1989 building was photographed on 29th August 2008. Passenger figures were steadily increasing and the future of the lines seemed secure. (B.W.L.Brooksbank)

MP Middleton Press

EVOLVING THE ULTIMATE RAIL ENCYCLOPEDIA

Easebourne Lane, Midhurst, West Sussex.
GU29 9AZ   Tel:01730 813169

www.middletonpress.co.uk   email:info@middletonpress.co.uk
A-978 0 906520 B- 978 1 873793 C- 978 1 901706 D-978 1 904474
E - 978 1 906008   F - 978 1 908174

All titles listed below were in print at time of publication - please check current availability by looking at our website - *www.middletonpress.co.uk* or by requesting a Brochure which includes our *LATEST* RAILWAY TITLES also our TRAMWAY, TROLLEYBUS, MILITARY and WATERWAYS series